KU-500-488

◀ *A painting of French ambassadors by Henry VIII's court painter, Hans Holbein.*

Hundreds of maps and engravings show us what Tudor life was like. Beautiful paintings show foreign ambassadors visiting Britain, dressed in splendid clothes and carrying with them the latest scientific inventions.

Millions of written words survive from Tudor times. There are secret state papers, sea captains' journals, even a few diaries. The words of William Shakespeare are recited in our theatres every night. Tudor street names survive. They do not make puddings in Pudding Lane any more, but the name lives on.

We even use Tudor expressions. Rich people in the sixteenth century gave silver spoons as christening gifts, and we still say a wealthy family's baby is 'born with a silver spoon in its mouth'.

We can share the Tudors' joy at discovering new countries by reading the journal of Sir Walter Raleigh: 'The birds towards the evening singing on every tree with a thousand several tunes, cranes and herons of white, crimson and carnation perching on the river's side.'

A wreck raised from the sea off Portsmouth in 1982 was found to have preserved a glimpse of Tudor life. It was Henry VIII's warship, *Mary Rose*, which sank in 1545. We can now visit the restored ship and see 14,000 Tudor objects including weapons, pewter dishes, musical instruments, leather shoes and a backgammon set.

▶ *A Tudor painting of the* Mary Rose.

▲ Henry VIII, dressed in typical splendour.

▼ Hampton Court Palace, which Cardinal Wolsey presented to Henry VIII after the king grew jealous of its magnificence.

chapter two

WHO WERE
THE TUDORS?

The kings and queens of the Tudor family ruled England from 1485 to 1603. Henry Tudor of Lancaster won the crown at the Battle of Bosworth in 1485. This ended the Wars of the Roses in which two branches of the royal family, Lancaster and York, fought for the throne. Henry VII combined the two family emblems, the red rose of Lancaster and white rose of York, into the Tudor rose, shown above. It was a symbol of the newly unified country.

The fight for the Crown had bankrupted England. Henry VII now avoided costly wars and managed the country's money carefully. He wiped out England's debts and turned England into a wealthy world power.

Contents

NEATH PORT TALBOT LIBRARIES

chapter one

HOW DO WE KNOW ABOUT
THE TUDORS?

You can see the world of the Tudors all around you. It surrounds you as you walk through a great college entrance gate in Oxford or Cambridge, or stand looking up at a chapel ceiling decorated with elaborate fans of stone. In a town like Shrewsbury, you can walk down streets that look nearly as they did four hundred years ago.

In 1560, John Grene made an adjustable chair for Elizabeth I 'with cloth of gold and staies, springes and staples of iron to set the same higher and lower, with a pillow of down'.

▶ *Christ Church College, Oxford, built during the reign of King Henry VIII.*

In great palaces like Hampton Court, in London, you can imagine how rich and powerful Tudors lived. Tudor monarchs liked palaces. By the time he died, Henry VIII had fifty-five. Inside them, we can still see the Tudors' tapestries, silver candlesticks and fine furniture. Elizabeth I even had a chair with an adjustable back.

In 1509, Henry died and his son became King Henry VIII. The new king was a fine sportsman. He also claimed he could out-drink any of his courtiers. He ruled with extravagant displays of power, once leading 5,800 followers to France, to meet the French king at the Field of the Cloth of Gold. He had to raise taxes to pay for such exploits, and for his expensive wars with France and Scotland.

Henry VIII left the running of the country to powerful ministers like Cardinal Thomas Wolsey and, later, Thomas Cromwell. Wolsey became rich enough to build Hampton Court. This palace, which had 1,000 rooms and 280 silk-covered beds, is a striking part of our Tudor heritage.

▲ *This strange helmet was given to Henry VIII by the emperor of Germany, Maximilian I.*

Henry married six times. He divorced his first wife, Catherine of Aragon, after she failed to produce a son. Henry's divorce was opposed by the Pope, who controlled the Catholic Church in England. To get his own way, Henry passed the Act of Supremacy, appointing himself 'Supreme Head of the Church in England'. He could now run the English Church as he wished, with no interference from the Pope in Rome.

Desperate for a son to succeed him, Henry VIII married six times. His wives were Catherine of Aragon (divorced), Anne Bolcyn (beheaded), Jane Seymour (died giving birth to Henry's only son), Anne of Cleves (divorced), Catherine Howard (beheaded) and Catherine Parr (who survived him).

One state paper tells us that Henry VIII spent his time shooting, singing, dancing, wrestling, playing recorders and composing songs. Official accounts record that in December 1530, he spent £4,464, including £2000 on jewels and pearls.

Church and Crown

Henry VIII's only son, the sickly Edward VI, became king at the age of ten. He ruled for six years, but because he was so young the country was governed by a nobleman called the Lord Protector. During Edward's reign, the English Church adopted the new Protestant faith that had swept through Europe. The publication of the first *English Book of Common Prayer* helped to establish the new form of worship throughout the country.

In 1553, Mary, Henry VIII's daughter by Catherine of Aragon, inherited the Crown. Queen Mary tried to revive the Catholic Church in England, and married Philip II, the Catholic king of Spain. Her religious persecution of Protestants, during which 283 people were burnt at the stake, earned her the nickname 'Bloody Mary'.

When Mary died in 1558, Elizabeth, the Protestant daughter of Ann Boleyn, became queen. Elizabeth I ruled the country for forty-five years until 1603.

▲ *This splendid suit of armour was worn in tournaments by King Henry VIII.*

The courts of Tudor monarchs grew bigger and bigger. Henry VIII had about 800 courtiers; Elizabeth had 1500! Tudor monarchs went on 'progresses', from palace to palace. Elizabeth took 400 carts of luggage with her. The average speed of her progresses was under five kilometres an hour.

During Elizabeth's long reign, the country grew steadily wealthier. William Shakespeare wrote his plays. Sir Francis Drake made a voyage around the world. An attempted invasion by Spain in 1588 was foiled when the English Navy defeated the mighty ships of the Spanish Armada.

Elizabeth, like Mary, died without children. Her cousin, the Scottish king James Stuart, became James I of England. The end of Elizabeth's reign was the end of the Tudors.

Pope Sixtus V said of Queen Elizabeth: 'She is a great woman ... Look how well she governs, only mistress of half an island, yet she makes herself feared by Spain, by France, by the Emperor, by all.'

▲ *The magnificent court of Elizabeth I making a progress in 1600.*

▲ *This jewellery was recovered from a Spanish ship sunk during the defeat of the Armada.*

chapter three

HOW DID THE TUDORS FOUND **AN EMPIRE?**

England was a small and not particularly powerful European country in 1500. One hundred years later, it was a 'world power', with the beginnings of an empire.

From early Tudor times, explorers set out to find new countries with which to trade, and quicker routes to countries they knew. Many searched for a northern passage to China, either to the west, north of America, or to the east, north of Russia.

In 1497, five years after Christopher Columbus had discovered America, John Cabot, an Italian navigator, set sail from Bristol. Henry VII was his patron and his ship was paid for by local merchants. Cabot reached an island that he thought was China, but which was probably Newfoundland. He had not found Asia, but fishermen could now follow his route to Newfoundland each year, to bring back cod.

An explorer told Elizabeth I that he believed a North-East Passage to China existed because a unicorn's horn had been found on the northern coast of Russia. He said it must have floated there from China, where unicorns were thought to exist. So, there must be a sea route joining the two countries!

▶ *A Tudor compass.*

HEATH PORT TALBOT LIBRARIES

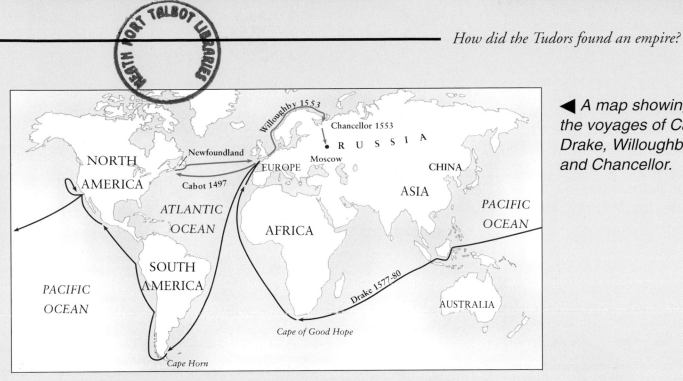

◀ *A map showing the voyages of Cabot, Drake, Willoughby and Chancellor.*

In 1553, Sir Hugh Willoughby and Richard Chancellor sailed in search of a passage to China, round the north of Russia. Willoughby was shipwrecked in Lapland, and froze to death. Chancellor reached Moscow, and met the Russian 'tsar', or king, Ivan the Terrible. Willoughby and Chancellor failed to find a route to China (it was finally found in the nineteenth century and is today kept open by Russian ice-breakers). They did, though, open a route for merchants and diplomats to travel regularly between Russia and England.

In September 1580, Francis Drake completed a three-year, round-the-world voyage. Drake's companions made written records of his exploits. They describe the many pirate raids Drake made against Spanish ships in the Pacific: 'We espied two ships under sail and gave chase to one ... We boarded her from the ship's boat without resistance. We found her to be a good prize, yielding us a good store of wine.'

From these Tudor expeditions grew the British 'world power', with its huge trading empire, of later times.

▼ *This cup held a coconut collected by Drake on his voyage.*

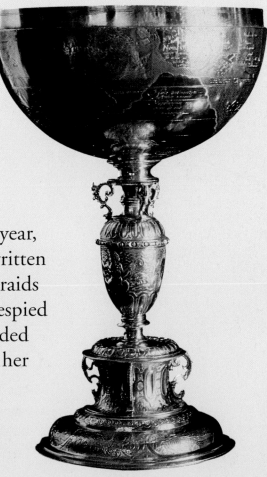

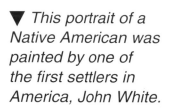

▼ *This portrait of a Native American was painted by one of the first settlers in America, John White.*

Colonies and Trade

Like the Vikings, Elizabethan sailors were also pirates, raiding and capturing ships carrying gold. Some were slave traders too. In 1562, Sir John Hawkins became the first Englishman to trade in slaves, shipping 300 Africans from Sierra Leone and trading them for hides, sugar and 'cochineal', a dye made from crushed insects.

During Tudor times, trade began with Turkey and countries of the eastern Mediterranean, then with India. Trading companies were founded, such as the Russian Company in 1555 and the East India Company in 1600. Trade helped English industry. After 1500, large quantities of cloth were sold abroad. A light cloth called worsted was exported to hot countries like Italy and Spain. Imports increased, including goods such as ivory, spices, silk, gold, furs and timber.

Traders were known as 'merchant adventurers'. Their expeditions were very risky. Ships were wrecked and taken by pirates. But that is how world sea trade began, and England grew powerful through the wealth that it brought. Merchants established trading stations that developed into the first 'colonies' – the beginnings of the British Empire.

In 1595, Sir Walter Raleigh set out to find gold along the Orinoco River, in South America. He found little treasure, but heard tales of kings covered in gold: 'They rub their naked bodies with sap to make them sticky. Then their servants take hollow sticks and blow powdered gold all over them until they are shining from head to foot.'

Queen Elizabeth gave Sir Walter Raleigh a charter 'to discover barbarous countries ... and to occupy and enjoy the same for ever'. Raleigh attempted to establish an American colony at Roanoke in Virginia, but every one of the 117 people who settled there in 1587 disappeared. Lessons were learnt, though. Soon after Elizabeth's reign, North American colonies began to survive and grow.

According to tradition, Raleigh brought back from Virginia the first potato plant ever seen in England. Raleigh also made pipe smoking fashionable. He had first bought tobacco from Francis Drake, who had traded it from Native Americans during his round-the-world voyage.

▲ *A seventeenth-century drawing of the potato plant.*

◀ *Raleigh's tobacco pouch, clay pipes and finger-shaped pipe stopper.*

▶ *An artist's impression of Raleigh's first ever smoke.*

A play written by Ben Jonson, and first performed at the Globe Theatre in 1598, mocks the new fashion of smoking clay pipes: 'I marvel what pleasure ... they have in taking this roguish tobacco; it's good for nothing but to choke a man, and fill him full of smoke and embers.'

chapter four

WHAT TUDOR BUILDINGS CAN WE STILL SEE?

▲ *The beautiful ceiling of King's College chapel, in Cambridge, completed during Henry VII's reign.*

The Tudors built palaces, houses and colleges in great numbers. Many survive. A palace like Hampton Court was a symbol of power and success. It first belonged to Cardinal Wolsey, but most of the present Hampton Court is the result of rebuilding by Henry VIII. The palace had running water, carried in lead pipes from under Coombe Hill, three miles away.

Partly to impress foreigners, but also to make sure his homes were as splendid as those of great churchmen, Henry VII had many houses built. There were seven royal homes near London at the start of his reign, and sixteen by 1509.

In 1531, Henry VIII built the largest palace in the Christian world at Whitehall, in London. It contained its own leisure centre with four tennis courts, a bowling alley and a jousting arena. At its centre was a 'cockpit', a magnificent building devoted to cockfights, on which Henry might bet as much as £5,000. The remains of the great palace are now hidden by the Cabinet Offices of the British Government.

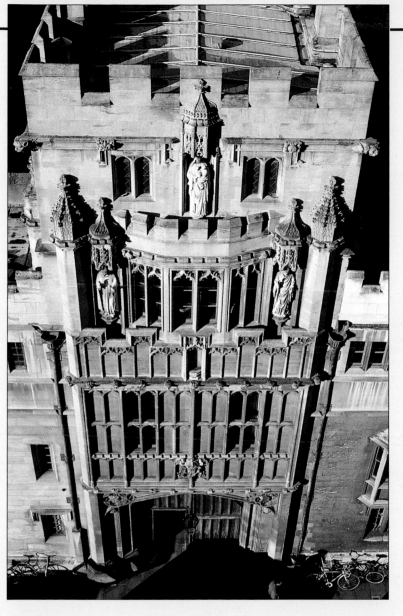

Building too grand a home could be seen as a threat to the king. Thomas Cromwell warned Wolsey: 'Sir, some there be that doth allege that Your Grace doth keep too great a house and family, and that ye are continually building ... I most heartily beseech Your Grace ... to refraine yourself, for a season, from all manner of building.'

◀ *The entrance gate to Brasenose College was built during the Tudor age.*

Colleges

The Tudor building boom produced many of the beautiful colleges that we can still walk through in Cambridge and Oxford. In Oxford, Corpus Christi and Brasenose Colleges were built between 1500 and 1520. In Cambridge, Jesus, Christ's, St John's, and Magdalene Colleges are all Tudor.

The beauty of some college buildings, like the chapel of King's College in Cambridge, is breathtaking. The architect, John Wastell, also designed the Henry VII Chapel in Westminster Abbey. Both buildings were worked on by teams of master craftsmen. But the use of a single architect to direct the plans was a Tudor invention.

The poet John Skelton commented on the fashion for buildings designed for show: 'Building royally, their mansions curiously, with turrets and with towers, with halls and with bowers, stretching to the stars.'

▲ *Tudors planted colourful 'knot gardens', like this reconstructed one at New Place, in Stratford-upon-Avon.*

The first English book on architecture, John Shute's *First and Chief Groundes of Architecture*, comes from Tudor times. It is not very practical. Shute says that the architect should study not only buildings, but grammar, philosophy, physics and music.

Houses

Life was more peaceful in 1550 than in 1480. Castles and defences were not really needed. A great deal of stone became available cheaply after 1536, when Henry VIII ordered the country's monasteries to be pulled down. So, well-off Tudor people built and built, and many of their buildings – the greatest mansions and large houses – survive. Some are still lived in.

We can visit luxurious Tudor houses such as Longleat, in Wiltshire, and Hardwick Hall, in Derbyshire. A tour of a great house shows us that life for some people in Britain was becoming more comfortable. Rooms had ornate ceilings of plaster and great chimney pieces in carved stone. Architects used beautifully carved wood, both to decorate the outside of the house and for fine panelling inside.

Interior walls were sometimes painted, and hung with portraits and tapestries. By the end of the century there were water closets (lavatories) in some houses – a very important part of our heritage! By 1600, the English had begun to develop a modern taste for luxury.

Hundreds of smaller Tudor houses still dot the countryside. Manor houses and fine farmhouses were built in different styles for different parts of the country.

In towns like Chester and Shrewsbury, whole streets of white and black, timber-framed Tudor buildings still exist. 'Mock Tudor' houses – modern versions of Tudor buildings – are still being built. Sometimes, they have black paint where real Tudor houses would have had black timbers.

Erasmus, a Dutch scholar, described a Tudor home: 'The floors are made of clay and are covered with layers of rushes, constantly replenished, so that the bottom layer remains for twenty years harbouring spittle, vomit, the urine of dogs and men, the dregs of beer, the remains of fish, and other nameless filth.'

▼ *Little Moreton Hall, in Congleton, Cheshire, is a fine example of a timber-framed Tudor house.*

chapter five

WHAT DO WE KNOW ABOUT
TUDOR LIFE?

The Tudors wrote books of 'marriage guidance'. A husband was warned that to 'cause injury to his wife by word or deed' would be 'as if he should spit into the air, and the same spittle return back upon himself'. Wives were warned not to call their husbands pet-names like 'Duck, chick, Pigsney'.

▼ *This engraving shows us how London looked in 1600.*

Documents tell us that for people of Tudor times, death was never far away. In 1563, one-sixth of the population of London died from plague. Diseases like smallpox and tuberculosis were often fatal. Most people carried weapons. Even the law was violent. People suspected of being witches were burnt, and in Edward VI's reign, an average of 560 people a year were hanged for various offences.

A quarter of the population of London was considered poor. Parishes gave out pensions of sixpence a week per person. Between 1541 and 1560, Londoners built thirty-seven almshouses to shelter the homeless. The present welfare state is perhaps our heritage from such Tudor charity.

THAMESIS

◀ *Elizabeth I, in 1592, wearing white make-up and the latest fashions.*

For the rich, fashion was of great importance. Paintings show Tudor gentlemen in ruffs (collars), embroidered breeches and silk stockings that are as colourful as women's styles. Children were also often dressed in these adult fashions.

Tudor women coloured their skin lily-white by using make-up made from white lead mixed with vinegar. At the end of her reign, Elizabeth I appeared 'painted not only all over her face, but on her neck and breasts also ... in some places near half an inch thick'.

Learning

The Tudors founded many new schools, some of them with money raised when Henry VIII closed down the country's monasteries. Scholars did their studying in Latin, the language used for writing and often speaking. Subjects included science, law, medicine, grammar and arithmetic.

In 1500, few girls were taught to read and write, but by the end of Elizabeth's reign the literacy rate for women was as high as at any time until the nineteenth century. One Tudor man complained: 'Instead of song and music let them learn cookery and laundry.'

Scientific discoveries made in the sixteenth century changed the way that we think about the universe. In medieval times, it was thought that the planets revolved around the Earth. In 1543, the Polish astronomer Copernicus published a book which explained that the sun was in fact the centre of our universe.

▼ *A beautiful emerald watch, made in about 1600, discovered at Cheapside, London.*

19

Eating was a popular pastime in Tudor times. At the Field of the Cloth of Gold, Henry VIII's party consumed 1,140 cows, 2,220 sheep, 160,000 litres of beer and 125,000 litres of wine. The exotic menu included dolphin, porpoise, stork, bittern and egret.

▼ *The children of Lord Cobham enjoy a dessert of fruit, nuts and wine, watched by the family pets.*

Leisure

Tudor life was full of games and sport. Henry VIII liked royal tennis, a special indoor variety played in irregular-sided halls. He once gambled away £42 on a game. Royal tennis is still played, sometimes on the original courts.

We play other Tudor games, like hide and seek. Villages still have bowling greens, and the bowls have a 'bias' to make them swerve, which is a Tudor invention. The Tudors played football too, a rather violent kind with no pitch, no referee and no rules. Everyone just joined in – and it was illegal!

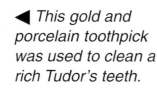

▲ This Tudor tennis ball was found in the rafters of Westminster Hall.

Today, sports like football and fencing are more civilized. Other Tudor games do not appeal to us, like shin-kicking or cudgel-play, which involved clattering your opponent with a wooden stick until the blood flowed.

Tudors enjoyed gambling on brutal sports such as bear-baiting and cockfighting. Such sports are now illegal, but sadly they still go on at a few secret locations. The Tudors also gambled on cards and dice. They invented whist and called it 'triumph', from which we get the word 'trumps'. Dice was popular, and so was cheating – 'bristled dice' had an invisible bristle on one face which affected the throw.

Fairs and games took place on Shrove Tuesday and other Church 'holy days'. These came to be called 'holidays', as they still are.

Fun and games made people thirsty. There was no tea or coffee then, and most water was undrinkable. There was also no whisky, gin or brandy. Most people, even children, drank weak beer called ale. The word 'ale' also meant a gathering where beer was drunk. A 'cuckoo-ale' was held to celebrate hearing the first cuckoo of the year.

◄ This gold and porcelain toothpick was used to clean a rich Tudor's teeth.

Archbishop Cranmer recorded his boat passing Henry VIII's royal barge, which was 'baiting of bears in the water'. The bear 'broke loose ... and came into the boat', pushing Cranmer out. It was recaptured by Henry: 'Away with the bear'.

chapter six

WHAT WERE THE TUDORS'
RELIGIOUS BELIEFS?

When Henry VIII became king, the Church in England was Catholic. At its head was the Pope, who controlled religious affairs in England from Rome. But by the time Henry died, he himself had become supreme head of the Church in England. It had become an English Church.

Sir Thomas More refused to recognize Henry as head of the Church. He said: 'I am accused of breaking the law made by Parliament. But I say that the law goes against God's law and the law of the Church. Therefore, I must not obey it. No-one can change God's law, and only the Pope can change the Church's law.'

This change arose from Henry's 'great matter' – he wanted the Pope to divorce him from Catherine of Aragon, so that he could marry Anne Boleyn. The Pope refused. So, Henry persuaded Parliament to pass a law making him head of the Church. This meant that the English bishops now served the king rather than the Pope. Henry could now obtain his divorce from them.

It was an important change. It meant no more religious rule from outside the country. The monarch was now more powerful than before.

Henry ordered that everyone should take the Oath of Supremacy, pledging loyalty to the king as head of the Church. Some refused, like the writer and statesman Sir Thomas More, who was beheaded for treason.

◀ *Sir Thomas More, who was beheaded for refusing to recognize Henry VIII as head of the Church of England.*

▲ *Pope Clement VII, who refused to grant Henry his divorce.*

The Monasteries

The Church owned over a fifth of the country's land. Its monasteries were very wealthy, and Henry needed their riches to pay for his wars. There were huge numbers of monks, and they did not always lead very religious lives. Henry used this as an excuse to dissolve, or abolish, the monasteries.

The land, buildings and treasures of the monasteries were simply handed over to the Crown. Works of art disappeared. Abbots who hid their silver were executed.

State papers record Royal officials using violence to dissolve Langdon Priory in Kent: 'I stood a great space knocking at the abbot's door. I found a short poleaxe and with it I dashed the abbot's door to pieces. And about the house I go with the poleaxe in my hand, for the abbot is a dangerous knave.'

▼ *The abbot of the richest monastery, Glastonbury Abbey, was hanged here on Glastonbury Tor.*

Ruins of some of these monasteries still stand. Others have gone. Lewes Abbey was flattened with explosives. Some were converted into houses, like that of Sir Francis Drake in Buckland, Devon. The abbeys of Chester, Gloucester and Westminster survive as cathedrals.

▲ *The first English Bible, translated by William Tyndale, was published in 1525.*

▼ *The execution of Lady Jane Grey in 1553.*

Protestantism

People by this time had developed 'Protestant' beliefs. They wanted their Bible and services to be in English, not the Latin used by Catholic priests. They wanted to pray to God without using complicated rituals.

Edward VI was a devout Protestant. During his reign, the *English Book of Common Prayer* was written by the Archbishop of Canterbury, Thomas Cranmer. Edward ordered its use in churches, but Catholics resisted such changes. This was the beginning of a violent struggle between two Christian beliefs that has gone on ever since.

Edward was succeeded by his Catholic sister Mary. Her first act was to execute Lady Jane Grey, who some noblemen had tried to make queen because she was a Protestant. It was the start of Mary's bloody attempts to revive the Catholic faith.

Mary ordered three leading Protestants, Cranmer, Nicholas Ridley and Hugh Latimer, to be burnt at the stake in Oxford, in 1555. But her cruelty only strengthened support for Protestant beliefs.

The famous words of the Protestant martyr Nicholas Ridley before his execution have become part of our religious heritage: 'We shall this day light such a candle by God's grace in England, as I trust shall never be put out.'

◀ *The burning of Ridley and Latimer, from John Foxe's* Book of Martyrs.

Elizabeth's Anglican Church

When Elizabeth I became queen, she wanted to end the bloodshed caused by religious arguments. She wanted the English Church to be strong. Elizabeth revived the English Bible and Prayer Book, but added changes to make Catholics more likely to accept it.

Elizabeth finished what Henry VIII had begun, creating an English Church – the Anglican Church. It was a combination of Protestant and Catholic beliefs, without the influence of Rome. From now on, reading the Bible and praying at home, without a priest, became part of an English Christian religion.

During Mary's reign, John Foxe wrote the *Book of Martyrs*. He described the sufferings of Protestants and illustrated the book with horrific woodcuts of people burning. It became a best-seller in Elizabethan times.

chapter seven

WHAT ARTS DID THE TUDORS LEAVE US?

William Shakespeare said that his poetry would last longer than anything: 'Not marble, nor the gilded monuments of princes shall outlive this powerful rhyme.' He was right to be confident about the lasting power of his language. His characters – Hamlet, Romeo and Juliet, Lady Macbeth, Richard III, Othello and many more – appear on stage every night in most countries of the world.

Sir Thomas More's wonderful book, *Utopia,* was a Tudor best-seller. It describes an ideal world in which there is no crime or poverty and every child has an education. People also wrote about the growing empire. A book by Richard Hakluyt collected together some amazing true and far-fetched tales of travel. Many soldiers and explorers, like Sir Philip Sidney and Sir Walter Raleigh, were poets whose works are still read.

The Tudors left us their music. 'Greensleeves' is a famous sixteenth-century tune, which some people believe Henry VIII composed. Like today, Elizabeth's reign was a great time for popular songwriting, with the singer usually playing a type of guitar called a lute.

▲ *A portrait of Shakespeare in 1610.*

In a poem probably written about Anne Boleyn, Sir Thomas Wyatt advises others not to fall in love with her. Round her neck, he writes, is a chain that says: '*Noli me tangere*, for Caesar's I am.' Don't touch me, I'm the king's!

◀ *The Globe Theatre, as it looked when it was built in Southwark in 1598 for Shakespeare's theatre company.*

In Shakespeare's famous play *Richard II*, the character John of Gaunt describes England as: 'This happy breed of men, this little world, This precious stone set in the silver sea.'

One of the greatest contributions to our heritage was the introduction of the printing press, just before Tudor times, by William Caxton. His work was carried on by Wynkyn de Worde, who published over 600 books before his death in 1535. Before this time, all books were handwritten and only available to the rich. Now, books poured from the printing presses, and became a part of daily life.

▼ *A modern actor performs at the opening of the reconstructed Globe in 1996.*

Mass-produced books were available to everyone. The effect was amazing. The printing press made knowledge available to the poor. It printed English translations of books by classical authors like the Greek poet Homer. It also produced the cheap Bibles and religious leaflets that made the spread of Protestantism possible.

chapter eight

WHAT LEGACIES REMAIN FROM TUDOR TIMES?

The Tudors still influence us in many ways. Organizations we value were founded in Tudor times. The Church of England was created. The Royal Navy was strengthened. In 1547, Trinity House was founded, which controlled the lighthouses and lightships around our coasts until 1995.

In some ways, modern politics began in Tudor times. Parliament was used to make more and more laws. In the war with Spain, Elizabeth regularly had to ask Parliament for money. As a result, the power of Parliament grew.

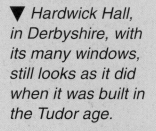

▼ *Hardwick Hall, in Derbyshire, with its many windows, still looks as it did when it was built in the Tudor age.*

◀ A sixteenth-century silver cup.

The Tudors improved domestic comfort. The first water closet was invented by Sir John Harington. Much more glass began to be used in houses. Beds had comfortable bedlinen, rooms had fireplaces. Meals were eaten off pewter plates, not wooden ones.

There were many other Tudor 'firsts': the first patents, the first guidebook, the first county histories, the first road maps and the first atlas of England – which was also the first national atlas in the world. Elizabeth even authorized the first public lottery, with prizes of cash and goods. Long before railways, came the Tudor idea of wooden tracks for coal-wagons. The Tudors passed the first laws to make new waterways and keep rivers like the Thames clear for navigation.

For some people, the most precious inheritance of the sixteenth century is the English language. Its words come from all over the world. Travellers and explorers brought back new words such as 'breeze', 'drill' and 'contraband'. English has been called the richest language in the world. The words of Shakespeare's plays offer strong evidence of this. The production of cheap books meant that this language could now be learnt and enjoyed by everyone.

It was a time of beginnings. Perhaps it was the beginning of our modern world. The British sense of being a 'great power' began in Tudor times. A pride in being British has lasted into this century.

Freedom of speech is a vital part of our heritage. In 1575, Peter Wentworth said of Parliament: 'Liberty of free speech is the only salve to heal all the sores of this commonwealth ... and without it, it is a mockery to call it a Parliament House.'

GLOSSARY

Almshouses Houses offering shelter to the old and poor.

Ambassadors State representatives sent to other countries.

Armada The Spanish fleet that attacked England in 1588.

Backgammon A popular dice and gambling game for two players.

Bankrupted Used up all the money of someone or something.

Breeches Trousers reaching to the knee.

Catholic The branch of the Christian Church ruled by the Pope.

Charter A state document giving permission or rights.

Colonies Settlements abroad ruled by the settlers' original country.

Courtiers Members of a monarch's court.

Diplomats Officials who deal with foreign affairs.

Empire Lands ruled by one country.

Exported Sent abroad for sale.

Gilded Covered in gold.

Imports Goods bought from abroad.

Jousting A sport in which two knights fight with lances on horseback.

Literacy The ability to read and write.

Martyrs People killed for refusing to give up their faith or belief.

Patents Grants protecting someone's right to sell their invention.

Patron Someone who offers support or money to a person or cause.

Persecution Mistreatment of a particular race, religion or group.

Pewter A metal made from lead and tin.

Plague A highly contagious disease.

Poleaxe A weapon with an axe blade and a spike.

Protestant The branch of the Christian Church that separated from the Catholic Church.

Replenished Renewed, refilled.

Rituals A set of procedures or ceremonies always performed in the same way.

Salve Something that heals.

Tapestries Pictures formed by weaving or embroidery.

Treason Betrayal of your own country or monarch.

Vikings Scandinavian sailors who raided across Europe from the eighth to the eleventh centuries.

Welfare state A government system of insurance and pensions designed to support people in need.

Woodcuts Pictures carved into a block of wood.

BOOKS TO READ

Childs, Alan *The History Detective Investigates: Tudor Home* (Wayland, 2002)
Childs, Alan *The History Detective Investigates: Tudor Theatre* (Wayland, 2002)
Cooper, Donna & Cliftlands, Bill *Tudors and Stuarts* (BBC Factfinder, 1993)
Deary, Terry *The Terrible Tudors* (Scholastic, 1993)
Hepplewhite, Peter *The History Detective Investigates: Tudor War* (Wayland, 2002)
Honey, Alison & Stevenson, Peter *Investigating the Tudors* (National Trust, 1993)
Ruby, Jennifer *The Tudors in Costume* (Batsford, 1995)
Weinstein, Rosemary *Tudor London* (Museum of London, 1994)

PLACES TO VISIT

There are Tudor buildings you can visit throughout Britain. Try to find out if there are any near your home. You might like to travel to the following places:

Tower of London, Tower Hill, London. Tel: 0870 756 6060
You can visit the Bloody Tower, where Sir Walter Raleigh, Lady Jane Grey and Anne Boleyn were all held Prisoner.

Hampton Court Palace, Hampton Court Road, London. Tel: 0870 751 5175
This magnificent Tudor palace built around a series of courtyards contains the great hall, astronomical clock and tennis courts built for Henry VIII.

Oxford and Cambridge Colleges. There are organized tours in both towns with guides to tell you the history of famous colleges built in Tudor times.

Mary Rose, Portsmouth, Hampshire. Tel: 023 9275 0521
You can visit the preserved wreck of Henry VIII's warship, and the many items from Tudor life that were recovered from it.

Hardwick Hall, near Mansfield, Derbyshire.
This Elizabethan mansion has so many windows that pople used to speak of 'Hardwick Hall, more glass than wall'. The beautiful rooms contain Tudor paintings and tapestries.

INDEX

Numbers in **bold** refer to pictures.

Picture acknowledgements
The publishers would like to thank the following for permitting the reproduction of their pictures: Bridgeman Art Library 9(top), 13(bottom-right), /Fitzwilliam Museum, University of Cambridge *cover*(left), 29, /Wallace Collection, London *cover*(bottom), 13(bottom-left), /National Gallery, London 5(top), 24(bottom), /Walker Art Gallery, London 6(top), /Guildhall Library, Corporation of London 18, /Frick Collection, New York 22, /Galleria Nazionale de Capodimonte, Naples 23(top), /British Museum, 24(top); ET Archives 1, 20, 25; Eye Ubiquitous 4, 23(bottom); Robert Harding 6(bottom), 16; Michael Holford 2, 3, 10, 12, 14, 21(bottom); Museum of London *cover*(right), 19(bottom), 21(top); Masters and Fellows, Magdalene College, Cambridge 5(bottom); National Portrait Gallery 19(top), 26; National Trust *cover*(centre), 17, 28; Oxford Picture Library 15; Ann Ronan 13(top); Board and Trustees, Royal Armouries 7, 8; Topham 11, 27(bottom); Ulster Museum, Belfast 9(bottom); Wayland Picture Library /Richard Hook 27(top). The map on page 11 is by Peter Bull Design.